TOOLS FOR TEACHERS

- **ATOS:** 0.6
- **GRL:** A
- **WORD COUNT:** 31

- **CURRICULUM CONNECTIONS:** animals, insects, nature

Skills to Teach

- **HIGH-FREQUENCY WORDS:** a, an, I, see
- **CONTENT WORDS:** ant, bee, beetle, butterfly, cricket, fly, insects, moth
- **PUNCTUATION:** periods
- **WORD STUDY:** consonant cluster *cts* (*insects*); broad /o/ (*moth*); multisyllable words (*beetle*, *butterfly*, *cricket*); compound word (*butterfly*)
- **TEXT TYPE:** information report

Before Reading Activities

- Read the title and give a simple statement of the main idea.
- Have students "walk" though the book and talk about what they see in the pictures.
- Introduce new vocabulary by having students predict the first letter and locate the word in the text.
- Discuss any unfamiliar concepts that are in the text.

After Reading Activities

Ask children to think of other insects they know of that were not named in the text. Write their answers on the board. Then invite them to discuss their experiences with the named insects. Have they seen the insects? Or have they just read about them in books? Tally the number of children who have seen each insect alongside its name. Which insects are the most commonly seen? Which are the least?

Tadpole Books are published by Jump!, 5357 Penn Avenue South, Minneapolis, MN 55419, www.jumplibrary.com

Copyright ©2018 Jump! International copyright reserved in all countries. No part of this book may be reproduced in any form without written permission from the publisher.

Editorial: Hundred Acre Words, LLC   **Designer:** Anna Peterson

Photo Credits: 123RF: Petr Podzemny, 10–11. Adobe Stock: Alekss, 2–3. Alamy: Alan Williams, 12–13; Domiciano Pablo Romero Franco, 4–5. Shutterstock: Cathy Keifer, 6–7; Dave Nelson, 14–15; Sayanjo65, 8–9; vnlit, 1; yothinpi, cover.

Library of Congress Cataloging-in-Publication Data
Names: Mayerling, Tim, author.
Title: I see insects / by Tim Mayerling.
Description: Minneapolis, Minnesota : Jump!, Inc., (2017) | Series: Outdoor explorer | Audience: Ages 3–6. | Includes index.
Identifiers: LCCN 2017023255 (print) | LCCN 2017034477 (ebook) | ISBN 9781624967184 (ebook) | ISBN 9781620319390 (hardcover: alk. paper) | ISBN 9781620319406 (pbk.)
Subjects: LCSH: Insects—Juvenile literature.
Classification: LCC QL467.2 (ebook) | LCC QL467.2 .M367 2017 (print) | DDC 595.7—dc23
LC record available at https://lccn.loc.gov/2017023255

OUTDOOR EXPLORER

I SEE INSECTS

by Tim Mayerling

TABLE OF CONTENTS

tadpole
books

I SEE INSECTS

I see a beetle.

I see an ant.

I see a moth.

I see a fly.

I see a cricket.

bee

I see a bee.

I see a butterfly.

WORDS TO KNOW

ant

bee

beetle

butterfly

cricket

fly

INDEX